ANIMALS ARE AMAZING

SHARKS

BY VALERIE BODDEN

This edition 2013

First published in the UK in 2012 by
Franklin Watts
338 Euston Road
London NW1 3BH

Franklin Watts Australia
Level 17/207 Kent Street
Sydney NSW 2000

First published by Creative Education,
an imprint of the Creative Company.
Copyright © 2010 Creative Education

ISBN 978 1 4451 2734 7
Dewey number: 597.3

A CIP catalogue record for this book
is available from the British Library.

Printed in China

Franklin Watts is a division of
Hachette Children's Books
an Hachette UK company
www.hachette.co.uk

Book and cover design by The Design Lab
Art direction by Rita Marshall

Photographs by 123RF (cbpix, Kristian Sekulic),
Alamy (Mark Conlin, Stephen Frink Collection),
Corbis (Ralph A. Clevenger), Dreamstime
(Afarusi119, Melvinlee), Getty Images (Brandon
Cole, Stephen Marks, Brian J. Skerry), iStockphoto
(Don Bayley, Dave Raboin), Minden Pictures
(Fred Bavendam)

CONTENTS

What are sharks?

Sharks swim in oceans all around the world.

Sharks are a type of fish. There are about 375 different kinds of sharks in the world. People are still **discovering** new kinds of sharks.

discovering finding for the first time.

Different sharks

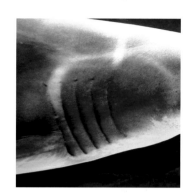

Sharks have rows of gills on each side of their head.

Sharks can be many colours. Some sharks are striped or spotted. Others are blue, grey or white. Sharks' **skeletons** are made of **cartilage** *(CAR-til-ij)* instead of bones. Sharks have lots of rows of sharp teeth. They breathe underwater through slits in their sides called gills.

cartilage a tough, bendy material in the body. People have cartilage in their nose and ears.
skeleton the hard frame inside a person or an animal.

Big sharks, little sharks

Sharks come in different sizes. The smallest sharks are the size of a child's hand. The biggest shark is the whale shark. It is longer than a bus! Whale sharks can weigh 18 tonnes. That is more than two African elephants put together!

The big whale shark eats only tiny fish and animals.

Ocean dwellers

Sharks live in every ocean of the world. Most sharks like to live in warm water. But some sharks, like the Great White, prefer to live in colder water. Many sharks live in **shallow** water near land. But some live in deep water in the middle of the ocean.

Many sharks like to hunt for food in shallow water.

shallow not deep.

Shark food

Most sharks eat fish and squid. Some really big sharks eat turtles, sea lions and dolphins. A few kinds of shark, such as the basking shark, eat **plankton**.

Some sharks like to find big groups of fish they can eat.

plankton a mixture of tiny floating plants and animals.

New sharks

Shark babies are called pups. Some mother sharks lay egg cases. An egg case can look a lot like a big seed pod. They are often called a 'mermaid's purse' because of their shape. Other sharks give birth to live babies.

Mother sharks leave the pups as soon as they are born, but sharks are very good at looking after themselves. Sharks can live for 20 to 30 years in the wild.

A shark pup comes out of its egg case when it has grown big enough to survive.

Sharks on the move

Sharks have to keep swimming all the time. Otherwise they will sink. This means that sharks can only sleep for a short time each day. Some sharks swim very far. They can swim thousands of kilometres every year!

Sharks move all the time but usually swim slowly.

Hunting for food

Sharks are top **predators**. They spend most of their time hunting for food. Lots of sharks hunt at night. They don't always need to see their **prey** because they can sense other fish moving through the water. Some kinds of sharks hunt alone. Others hunt in groups called **schools**.

Hunting sharks are good at smelling blood in the water.

predator an animal that eats other animals.
prey an animal that is eaten by other animals.
school a word used to describe a group of fish.

Sharks and people

People can get a close look at sharks in aquariums.

Many people are afraid of sharks. But most sharks will not hurt people. Most people will never see a shark in the ocean. But people can watch sharks at zoos and **aquariums** (*ah-KWARE-ee-ums*). It is exciting to see these strong fish swim through the water!

aquariums buildings where fish and other water animals are kept in big, glass tanks.

A shark story

Why do fishermen keep where they hunt for fish a secret?

People on the islands of Hawaii tell a story about this. They say that the King of Sharks had a son. He lived on land and he looked like a man. He asked the fishermen every day where they were going to hunt. The fishermen noticed that they were catching fewer fish and blamed the son. They chased him into the ocean and he turned back into a shark. Now the fishermen never tell anyone where they hunt in case the sharks find out!

Useful information

Read More

Leapfrog Learners: Sharks by Amelia Penn (Franklin Watts, 2013)

Animal Instincts: A Killer Shark by Tom Jackson (Wayland, 2013)

Amazing Animals: Sharks by Jen Green (Franklin Watts, 2013)

Websites

http://www.enchantedlearning.com/subjects/sharks
This site has lots of fascinating facts about sharks.

http://www.kidzone.ws/sharks
This site has shark facts, downloadable and online activities and lots of pictures of different types of shark.

http://kids.nationalgeographic.com/kids/animals/creaturefeature
Then type sharks into the search box to find lots of quizzes and facts about different types of sharks.

Every effort has been made by the Publishers to ensure that these websites are suitable for children, that they are of the highest educational value and that they contain no inappropriate or offensive material. However, because of the nature of the Internet, it is impossible to guarantee that the contents of these sites will not be altered. We strongly advise that Internet access is supervised by a responsible adult.

Index